Le

STAR POWERED BRAND

BECOME THE LUMINOUS LEADER
YOU WERE BORN TO BE

Star-Powered Brand / Leslie Tagorda

ISBN 978-1-953449-16-0

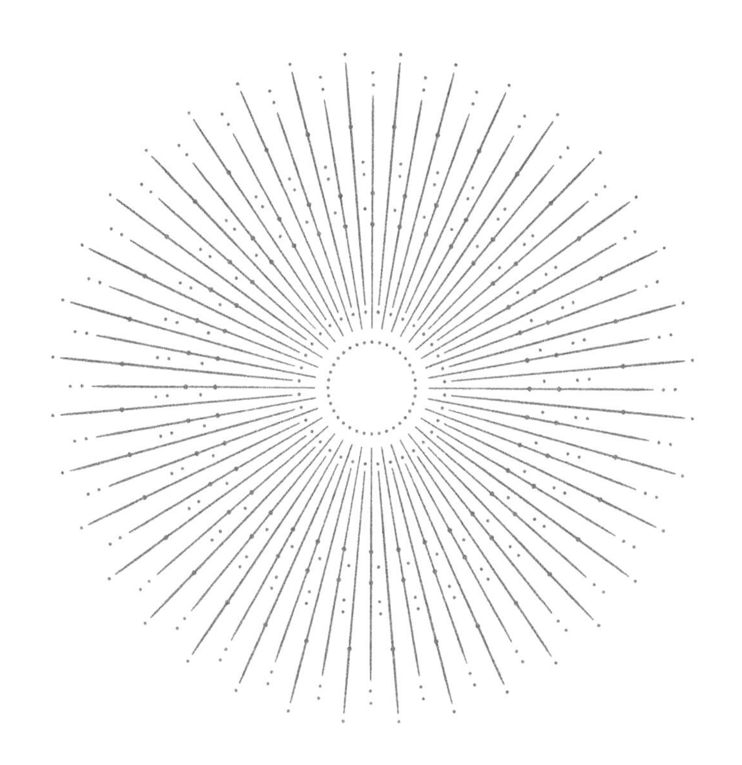

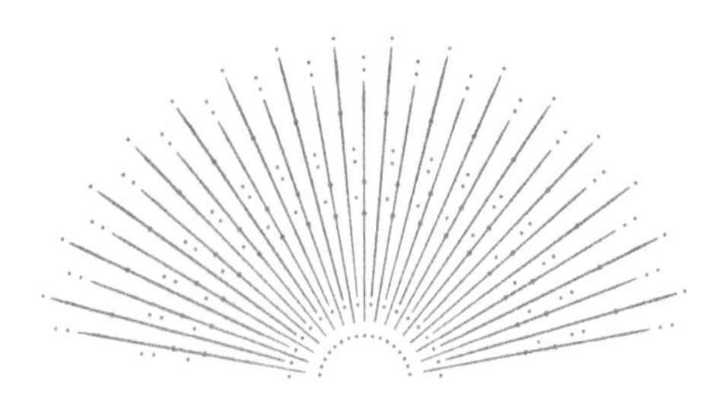

ODE TO YOU, LUMINARY ENTREPRENEUR

Moon and star gazers,
Inner truth seekers,
Lifelong explorers,
Equitable biz creators;

Inspired *action* takers,
Spiritual *thought* leaders,
Transformational *impact* healers,
And *freedom* life makers.

The time is *now* for you to **SHINE.**

LESLIE TAGORDA

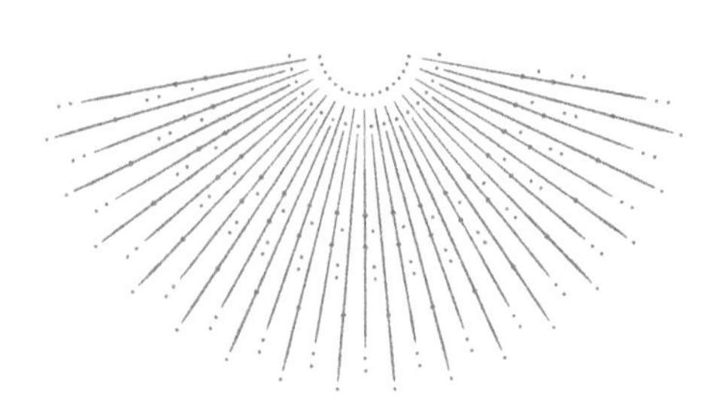

ACKNOWLEDGEMENTS

This book is dedicated to you, luminary.

Whether you are a successful entrepreneur reaching for even more, or a budding entrepreneur taking their first steps into the world of being your own boss.

This book is for you.

So you can:

- **Validate energies** we dismissed because of the "shoulds" we've unintentionally adopted.
- **Reveal superpowers** we dismissed because if it's so easy and natural for us, then everyone should be able to do it.
- **Decode soft powers** we repressed because we've been told it's too much, and not enough at the same time.
- **Amplify powers of attraction** we diluted because we try so hard to fit in but end up looking and acting like everyone else.

No natal chart is alike and there is no one else like you.

No one else can do what you do, in the way you do what you do.

xo,

Leslie Tagorda
Brand Astrologer and Designer

MAHALO

There are so many beautiful souls to thank for helping me to bring this tiny book into the world. While my path hasn't been straightforward, I couldn't wait to find a traditional publisher to bring this wisdom into the world.

Here are, in part, the wonderful people that have inspired and supported me.

Bevin, my astrology bestie that since 2005, we've collaborated and discussed business and astrology over decadent sushi dinners.

Aime Miyamoto and Milada Sakic, business astrologers and mentors that guided me and helped me validate the wisdom of the stars so long buried in me.

Asha Frost, Indiginous Medicine Woman, whose friendship and light, keep me going when things feel dark; reminding me of my path.

Suzanne Bellavista for helping me keep on track and editing away my very first book proposal. Some of her work appears in this tiny version. She's the eternal Cancerian cheerleader everyone needs.

To my vast community of friends, family and customers from around the globe, who love and believe in me. And who allow me to hold space for their dreams.

And lastly, to Jeff, my right hand person, by my side in my business for the last 10 years, traveling with me and growing with me, always being there when I need any little thing. This book and my business would not be possible without his help.

CONTENTS

ALOHA!

I believe that we are all luminaries, born to shine brightly and contribute our wisdom in the world.

And you, entrepreneur, have chosen a spiritual journey. The business you've created is an extension of your consciousness, born of the same energy as you. And meant to shine in your own unique way.

If you're like me, you've been taught to not trust in yourself and to not shine brightly. It's no wonder that we look outside ourselves to the "experts" to provide us with guidance that is already within us. We don't see ourselves as experts and we keep our brilliance dulled. Feeling not enough, and too much at the same time.

I'm here to teach you to access the guidance and insight that lives within you, the star-powers you were born with, so you can amplify and optimize that energy and show up uniquely yourself, without comparison or copying.

At the moment you were born, from that exact place on Mother Earth, the stars were in perfect alignment to imprint onto you the energies that power your life. These energies are a gift and you get to choose how to maximize those energies to shine more brilliantly in your life and business.

I hope that you will be able to use this book to reveal your one-of-a-kind star powers using your natal astrology. I want you to step up, step in, and step out with confidence and clarity in your own powers.
The world needs your mastery, and the best way for you to contribute your expertise is to stop hiding and shine brightly like the luminary you were born to be.

WHY BRAND AND BUSINESS ASTROLOGY?

I see a brand as the experience one has with your business.

Branding captures all those touch points, from your visual identity, to your customer service, to the way you share your ideas, to the leadership initiatives and the values you stand by.

We spend so much effort positioning our brand, hiring experts, following others in our field, and often getting stuck by comparison-kryptonite or not standing out because we look like everyone else!

There's a visionary and innovative way to lead your business, and it's already inside of you! Your astrology.

A VISIONARY'S WAY TO REVEAL THEIR ONE-OF-A-KIND BRAND

In branding, experts will craft detailed archetypes and psychographics based on modern psychoanalysis. But did you know, the founding father of psychoanalysis, Carl Jung—his research informing Myers Briggs personality tests and more—was a practicing Astrologer?

Western Astrology, an ancient tradition, was the original archetyping tool that wove divine mythos into the human experience. I call these zodiac-based archetypes "astrographics."

When we use astrology in our brand and business, we return full circle into understanding the divine within ourselves and expressing it outwardly into our purpose. As above, so below.

Most current brand and business strategists will recommend that an organization choose one brand archetype to create a connection and relationship with customers and fans.

There are no two luminaries alike, and like a luminary, no two people have the exact same astrological chart.

You are made of a specific blend that wants to come to the fore based on your primary foundational luminaries, your Sun, Moon, and Rising.

It is here that you will learn the different astrographics (astrology-based psychographics) and blend them to your unique star-powered design to become irresistibly, individually, you.

You will be able to make informed decisions that illuminate your business's distinct position, leadership, and style.

No copying, pretending, or comparing needed.

HOW TO EASILY DECODE YOUR STAR-POWER

READ YOUR SUN, MOON, AND RISING

Each of your luminaries (the Sun, Moon, and Rising) have different attributes. While we won't have the space to do full interpretations here, understanding these basic attributes and applying them to your luminaries will give you deep specifics and insights about your natural talents!

There are so many shiny objects in the solar system. Focusing and fine-tuning your core energies, your Sun, Moon and Rising, will set the foundation of your business and brand.

Like a musical instrument, the more in tune your fundamental energies, the higher vibration, the higher the resonance, and the higher your amplification. The more brightly you will shine.

ZODIAC SIGN

There are 12 different zodiacs in Western Astrology that are based on mythos and symbolism weaved into our human experience and culture. Each of the zodiacs are representations of a human archetype.

POLARITY

All 12 zodiacs are grouped into 6 pairs, called polarities. The pair act like magnets, desiring integration. You can't pull them apart; they create an axis of growth.

1. Relationship Axis: Aries - Libra
2. Financial Axis: Taurus - Scorpio
3. Communication Axis: Gemini - Sagittarius
4. Security Axis: Cancer - Capricorn
5. Purpose Axis: Leo - Aquarius
6. Service Axis: Virgo - Pisces

ELEMENT

The zodiacs are grouped into 4 groups of elements. The 4 elements are shared building blocks of humanity and life.

1. Fire: Yang, Creative, Imaginative, passionate, energizing Hot
   Aries, Leo, Sagittarius
2. Earth: Yin, Receptive, Patient, Building, Physical, Sensual, Solid
   Taurus, Virgo, Capricorn
3. Air: Yang, Social, Intellectual, Communicative, Fast, Fluid
   Gemini, Libra, Aquarius
4. Water: Yin, Receptive, Healing, Nurturing, Feeling, Emotional, Intuitive, Soft
   Cancer, Scorpio, Pisces

MODALITY

The zodiacs are grouped into 3 groups of modalities aka qualities. The 3 qualities are related to the type of action best suited.

1. Cardinal: The start of the season, begins a Solstice or an Equinox. Ignites things, takes initiative, gets the party started, has a vision. Needs help at following through or going with the flow.
   Aries, Cancer, Libra, Capricorn
2. Fixed: The middle of the season, you get deep into the season. Organizes, thorough, problem solving, investigative, stubborn, has a solution. Needs help at envisioning new ideas or changing direction.
   Taurus, Leo, Scorpio, Aquarius

3. Mutable: The end of the season, can see all options to go with the flow. Wisdom to see many perspectives, can easily change on a dime, will go where the wind blows. Needs help at taking initiative and getting to the bottom of things. *Gemini, Virgo, Sagittarius, Pisces*

HOUSE PLACEMENT

The natal chart is divided into 12 sections, similar to a piece of pie. Each of these sections represent an area in our life where the information of that energy is most readily available. You can look at these different slices with different filters, such as health and people. For our purposes, we are looking at these houses from the perspective of business and entrepreneurship.

When looked at from an entrepreneurship perspective, in a nutshell, the houses represent these areas in our business:

1H: Brand identity and leadership.
2H: Values, value add, and resources.
3H: Communications and marketing.
4H: Emotional security and safe spaces.
5H: Joy, creativity, pleasure, and purpose.
6H: Systems, day-to-day operations, and service to others.
7H: Commitments, soul customers, and partnerships.
8H: Shared resources, transformation, and shadows.
9H: Vision, public relations, philosophy, and exploration.
10H: Professional achievement, recognition, ultimate mission.
11H: Greater communities, networks, platforms, innovation.
12H: Restoration, reformation, retreat.

THE 12 HOUSES

where we experience business

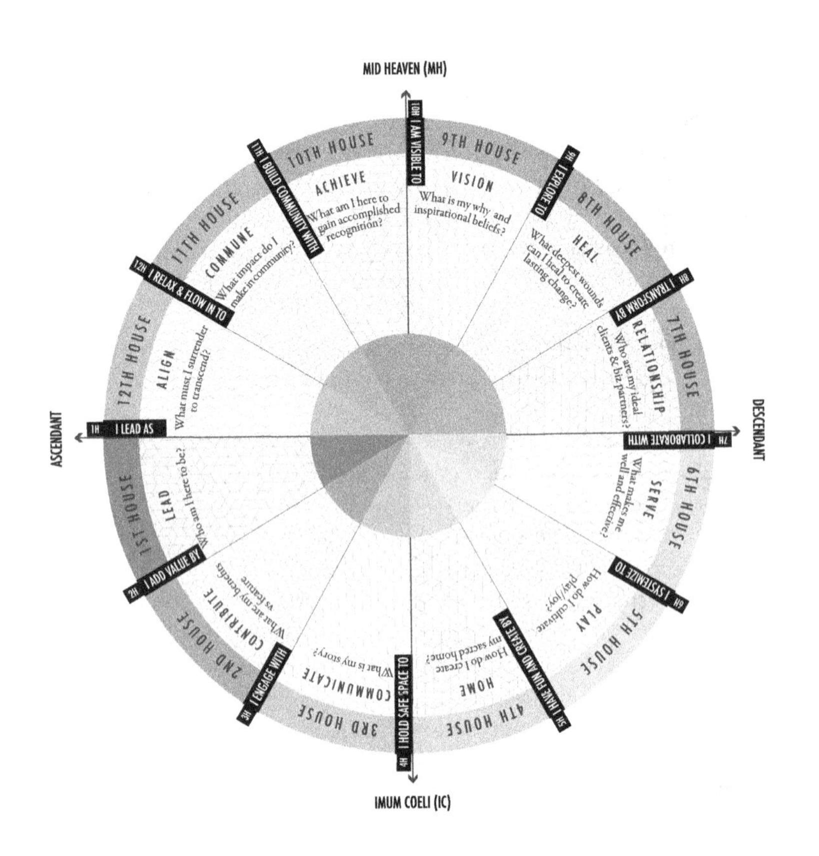

MAJOR ASPECTS

This is a bit of an advanced topic, yet I believe it's totally manageable. Most of your chart drawing software will show these aspects—the relationship between two or more energies in your chart. Generally the more exact the aspect, closer to the degree, the stronger the aspect will be.

In traditional astrology there are "good" and "bad" aspects....BUT... in your natal chart, everything is a *gift* for you to use in this life's evolution.

There is no judgement of good or bad when you can see the benefits and challenges of each relationship.

The rules below are general guidelines for you to use. For the simplicity of this book we are sticking to a 5° orb of energies

☌ Conjunction

Two energies that are near each other within 5° of each other.
The two energies are **blended** together, and cannot be separated.

☍ Opposition

Two energies that are opposite of each other at 180° (+/- 5° on either side).
The two energies want to be **integrated**; sometimes they work together, sometimes it feels like a struggle. They work best when both energies are given equal light.

□ Square

Two energies that are 45° of each other (+/- 5° on either side). The two energies will likely be in the same modality/quality. The energies will present each other **creative friction**. Understanding the tension between the energies will provide you the fuel you need to create great things with those energies. If you don't harness the energies and recognize them as fuel, they can show up as great challenges and frustrations.

△ Trine

Two energies that are 120° of each other (+/- 5° on either side). The two energies will likely be in the same element. The energies will support each other. They will work **in flow** with each other and feel easy - lucky even. Take note—if you have trines, because the energy is harmonious and easy, one can become complacent, not recognize their blessings and therefore not appreciate the gift. If you don't recognize your harmonious energies and luck, they go unnoticed and wasted.

INTRODUCING THE 12 ZODIAC ASTROGRAPHICS AND ARCHETYPES

Archetype, Astrographic, or Psychographics

You've likely heard from a brand or business strategists to choose one brand archetype so you can create a connection and relationship with customers. However, you are made up of all the archetypes and there is a specific blend that wants to come to the fore based on your primary foundational luminaries, your Sun, Moon, and Rising.

It is here that you will learn the different astrographics (astrology-based psychographics) and blend them to your unique star-powered design to become irresistibly, individually, you. No copying or comparing needed.

Spectrum of Expressions

Each zodiac lives on a spectrum, from low, shadow expressions, to high, light expressions.

You are already expressing your luminary (Sun, Moon, Rising) zodiacs and our lifetime goal is to raise the vibration of that expression. Especially in our business and the way we show up.

Planetary Ruler

Each of the zodiacs have a planetary ruler. If you have a planet you want to learn more about, find the zodiac for which it rules and adopt the energies of that zodiac to that planet.

RULERS

Mars

♂

♈

Aries

I AM

ARCHETYPE

The Warrior

HOPES + DESIRES

HIGH VIBRATION QUALITIES

I embrace my expertise + continue to grow into

Leadership, initiative, confidence, bravery, standing ground

PROBLEMS + FEARS

LOW VIBRATION QUALITIES

I can get stuck in + learn to let go of

Anger, frustration, ego, impulsivity, reactivity,

BE BOLD

ELEMENT

Fire (Inspire)

EXPRESSION

Ignite and Energize - Self

MODALITY

Cardinal

DESIRES

To be first,
to be noticed, to be seen,
to be recognized,
to be bold, to take risk

ARCHETYPE

Warrior, pioneer, explorer, combatant, freedom, fighter, defender, rescuer, worthy, opponent, dare devil, adventurer, newborn

RULERS

Venus

♀

ARCHETYPE

The Creator

Taurus

I HAVE

HOPES + DESIRES	PROBLEMS + FEARS
HIGH VIBRATION QUALITIES	**LOW VIBRATION QUALITIES**
I embrace my expertise + continue to grow into	**I can get stuck in + learn to let go of**
Stability, security, pleasure, sensuality, prosperity, practicality	Over indulgence to pleasures, hoarding, excessiveness

BE PEACEFUL

ELEMENT

Earth (Create)

EXPRESSION

Build and
Manifest - Worth

MODALITY

Fixed

DESIRES

To be secure,
to be comfortable,
to have pleasure

ARCHETYPE

Farmer, the nature spirit,
the musician, the silent one,
the object of passion,
the owner, the temptress,
the artist, the creator,
the banker

RULERS

Mercury

☿

Gemini

I THINK

ARCHETYPE

The Storyteller

HOPES + DESIRES	PROBLEMS + FEARS
HIGH VIBRATION QUALITIES	**LOW VIBRATION QUALITIES**
I embrace my expertise + continue to grow into	I can get stuck in + learn to let go of
Curiosity, listening, engaging, conversing, versatility, adaptability	Overthinking, overwhelm, indecisiveness

BE CURIOUS

ELEMENT

Air (Think)

EXPRESSION

Relate and Exchange Ideas - With Similar

MODALITY

Mutable

DESIRES

To be heard,
to be understood,
to engage

ARCHETYPE

Jester, student, storyteller, gypsey, wanderer, journalist, trickster, comedian, child, writer, teacher, messenger

RULERS

Moon

☽

Cancer

I FEEL

ARCHETYPE

The Nurturer

HOPES + DESIRES

HIGH VIBRATION QUALITIES

I embrace my expertise + continue to grow into

Kindness, acceptance, nurturer, compassion, tolerance, femininity, gentleness

PROBLEMS + FEARS

LOW VIBRATION QUALITIES

I can get stuck in + learn to let go of

Enabling exclusion, rescuing, family traps

BE CARING

ELEMENT

Water (Feel)

EXPRESSION

Sense and Restore - Feminine

MODALITY

Cardinal

DESIRES

To create a safe space, to be with family/friends that are family, to be safe

ARCHETYPE

Healer, psychic mother, invisible man, maiden, witch, counsellor, seductress, psychologist

RULERS

Sun

☉

Leo

I WILL

ARCHETYPE

The Ruler

HOPES + DESIRES

HIGH VIBRATION QUALITIES

I embrace my expertise + continue to grow into

Open heartedness, self-expression, confidence, spontaneity

PROBLEMS + FEARS

LOW VIBRATION QUALITIES

I can get stuck in + learn to let go of

Privilege, entitlement, drama

BE LIKABLE

ELEMENT

Fire (Inspire)

EXPRESSION

Ignite and Energize - Confidence

MODALITY

Fixed

DESIRES

To be confident,
to creatively play,
to be open hearted

ARCHETYPE

Protector, warrior, artist, actor, ruler, king, performer, golden child, healer, prophet, magician, king/queen, guardian

RULERS

Mercury

☿

Virgo

I ANALYZE

ARCHETYPE

The Healer

HOPES + DESIRES

HIGH VIBRATION QUALITIES

I embrace my expertise + continue to grow into

Health service, wellbeing, healing, efficiency, procedure, routine, humility

PROBLEMS + FEARS

LOW VIBRATION QUALITIES

I can get stuck in + learn to let go of

Martyrdom, self-doubt, perfectionist, worry, workaholism

BE HEALTHY

ELEMENT

Earth (Create)

EXPRESSION

Build and Manifest - Wellness

MODALITY

Mutable

DESIRES

To be healthy, to be healthy, to be productive

ARCHETYPE

Craftsperson, healer, perfectionist, servant, analyst, alchemist, messenger, martyr, nature spirit, naturopath

RULERS

Venus

♀

ARCHETYPE

The Peacemaker

Libra

I HARMONIZE

HOPES + DESIRES

HIGH VIBRATION QUALITIES

I embrace my expertise + continue to grow into

Gratitude, diversity, belief, optimism, generosity, ethics, exploration

PROBLEMS + FEARS

LOW VIBRATION QUALITIES

I can get stuck in + learn to let go of

Bluntness, close-mindedness, indulgence

BE SOCIAL

ELEMENT

Air (Think)

EXPRESSION

Relate and Exchange Ideas - With Partners

MODALITY

Cardinal

DESIRES

To be connected (to others) to be attractive, to balance / equalize / harmonize

ARCHETYPE

Lawyer, counsellor, socialite, lover, peacemaker, creator, seductress, flirt, minx, designer, mediator judge

RULERS

Mars + Pluto

Scorpio

I DESIRE

ARCHETYPE

The Alchemist

HOPES + DESIRES

HIGH VIBRATION QUALITIES

I embrace my expertise + continue to grow into

Trust, empowerment, emotional integrity, intensity, presence, deep transformation

PROBLEMS + FEARS

LOW VIBRATION QUALITIES

I can get stuck in + learn to let go of

Power over others, secrecy, shame, blame

BE POWERFUL

ELEMENT

Water (Feel)

EXPRESSION

Sense and Restore - Power

MODALITY

Fixed

DESIRES

To be loyal, to feel deeply, to trust

ARCHETYPE

Mystic, alchemist, detective, sorcerer, hypnotist, chemist, psychiatrist, witch, investigator, fortune teller, guardian, actor

RULERS

Jupiter

♃

Sagittarius

I SEE

ARCHETYPE

The Explorer

HOPES + DESIRES	PROBLEMS + FEARS
HIGH VIBRATION QUALITIES	**LOW VIBRATION QUALITIES**
I embrace my expertise + continue to grow into	**I can get stuck in + learn to let go of**
Gratitude, diversity, belief, optimism, generosity, ethics, exploration	Bluntness, close-mindedness, indulgence

BE GRATEFUL

ELEMENT

Fire (Inspire)

EXPRESSION

Ignite and Energize - Belief

MODALITY

Mutable

DESIRES

To explore,
to expand mind/life,
to make an impact

ARCHETYPE

Wanderer, explorer, professor, story teller, inspirer, guide, philosopher, benefactor, free spirit, visionary

RULERS

Saturn

♄

Capricorn

I ACHIEVE

ARCHETYPE

The Authority

HOPES + DESIRES

HIGH VIBRATION QUALITIES

I embrace my expertise + continue to grow into

Achievement, results, integrity, consistency, realization, systems

PROBLEMS + FEARS

LOW VIBRATION QUALITIES

I can get stuck in + learn to let go of

Controlling, cynicism, bitterness

BE TENACIOUS

ELEMENT

Earth (Create)

EXPRESSION

Build and Manifest - Perseverance

MODALITY

Cardinal

DESIRES

To achieve
to be recognized in success,
to commit

ARCHETYPE

Old soul judge, mentor, prime minister, the father, entrepreneur, banker, wizard, builder

RULERS

Saturn +
Uranus

♄ + ♅

♒

Aquarius

I KNOW

ARCHETYPE

The Revolutionary

HOPES + DESIRES

HIGH VIBRATION QUALITIES

I embrace my expertise + continue to grow into

Individuality, social change
equality, freedom,
innovation, progress,
community

PROBLEMS + FEARS

LOW VIBRATION QUALITIES

I can get stuck in + learn to let go of

Chaos, alienation,
aloofness

BE FREE

ELEMENT

Air (Think)

EXPRESSION

Relate and Exchange
Idea - With Community

MODALITY

Fixed

DESIRES

To be unique and
unconformist,
to be innovative,
to separate emotionally

ARCHETYPE

Revolutionary, scientist, eccentric, visionary, rebel genius, outlaw, free spirit, activist, inventor, alchemist, teacher

RULERS

Jupiter +
Neptune

♃ + ♆

Pisces

I BELIEVE

ARCHETYPE

The Dreamer

HOPES + DESIRES

HIGH VIBRATION QUALITIES

I embrace my expertise + continue to grow into

Ease, inspiration, spirituality, wonder, interconectedness

PROBLEMS + FEARS

LOW VIBRATION QUALITIES

I can get stuck in + learn to let go of

Self-sacrifice, addiction, avoidance

BE RELAXED

ELEMENT

Water (Feel)

EXPRESSION

Sense and Restore – Spirituality

MODALITY

Mutable

DESIRES

To be relaxed at ease, to be compassionate, to be connected to spirit

ARCHETYPE

Mystic, dreamer, artist, poet, guide, guru, medic, healer, worshipper, creator, dancer, psychotic, addict, visionary, martyr

Radiate Your Brand's Superpowers

SUN SIGN IN YOUR BRAND

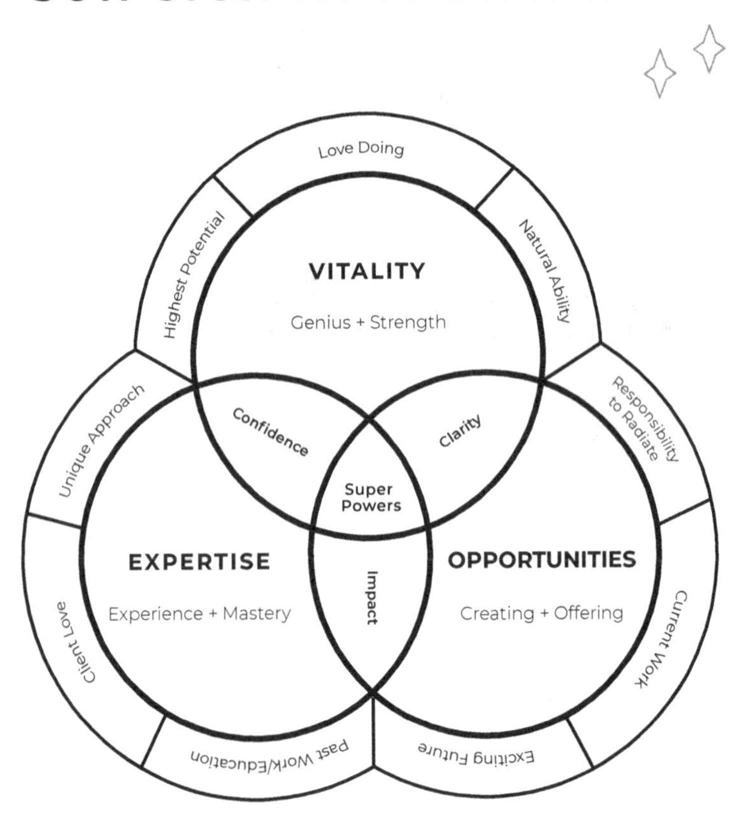

Your sun sign is the vital essence of your brand. The way you do what you do, that no one else can do just like you. It's at the soul level.

Sol—the latin spelling of the Sun. Your soul, the sun personified in you.

You see, there is no one else like you.

Our Sun sign represents what we do, how we do it, our mastery, and our brilliance. It's our superpowers.

Because our superpowers come so naturally to us we often dismiss it, assuming that if we're good at it, others are good at it too.

And that is our biggest mistake...

...To not recognize our superpowers, the secret sauce and experience we bring to doing what we love to do at our soul level.

When we don't acknowledge our expertise and mastery, we sell our value short. If we can't see our value, no one else will.

But magic happens when we can recognize our soul-level star-power.

We gain confidence in what we do well.

We gain clarity in how we do what we do so well.

And we gain impact because we amplify our expertise by focusing on our innate talent.

This comes with great responsibility: the responsibility to create opportunities that allow us to shine in our brilliance and confidently contribute our superpowers with the world.

What if you could recognize and own your genius and abilities?

What if you could distill the mastery you've always been using in your work?

What if you could define your exact expertise and your secret sauce—the way you do what you do?

Imagine knowing that what you do, in the way you do it, no one can do just like you.

Natural Ability
I recognize my abilities as unique superpowers.

- What you love to do
- What work feels so easy
- What you're amazing at

Expertise + Mastery
I know my expertise and how it differentiates me from others.

- Your past experiences
- Your education and expertise
- Your unique approach
- What past clients say about you

Creative Opportunities
I create opportunities and experiences that allow me to express my superpower.

- What you need to continue to amplify
- Opportunities you need to create for yourself
- Definition of your secret sauce

5 WAYS TO RADIATE YOUR SUPERPOWERS WITH YOUR SUN SIGN

✧ **Acknowledge Your Superpowers**
When you recognize your superpowers you gain confidence and clarity in what you uniquely do so well. We spend so much time dismissing our superpowers, assuming that others can do what we do. This kind of thinking doesn't up your value. Communicate your expertise and revel in your value, as there is no one who can do what you do just like you do!

✧ **Exude Your Genius**
When you are confident and clear you want to be seen and you show up in your genius! You don't need to be flashy or an influencer to exude your genius. Up-level your offers by focusing and expressing your genius and how it shows up in what you do.

✧ **Count Your Past Mastery**
When you really appreciate and take notice of the accomplishments you have achieved and listen to what others remark about your work, this adds to your creative value. It doesn't matter if your compliments and accomplishments come from roles many positions ago, all that you have done adds a special and unique flavor to your super-powered secret sauce. Collect and receive those compliments and share it with the world.

✧ **Incorporate Your Expertise**
By now, you've had many different jobs and roles and educational experiences. These are all significant to your approach and unique way of doing things. Do not discount any past expertise or experience; you never know who will be astounded by your past. Work this expertise into your unique process and approach to make your work one-of-a-kind.

✧ **Amplify your opportunity**
When you love what you do and clearly recognize your unique creative abilities, it's time to optimize and amplify. Focus your work by creating more opportunities to allow yourself to work in your superpower to do your best work. This allows for further mastery and building your confidence and brilliance to shine brighter.

SUPERPOWER YOUR SUN SIGN

1. Zodiac Sign
This is the core archetypal energy that you need to be creatively expressing.
Radiate this solar energy in everything you do and master.

2. House Placements
Whichever house your sun is in will give you insight as to what area of your business your creative expression wants to express itself fully.

I create opportunities in my brand so I may work my Sun's superpowers in...

1H: My brand identity and leadership role.
2H: Building wealth, worth and value.
3H: Communicating, social media, and teaching others.
4H: Building a legacy, safe community and home.
5H: Passionate, fun, creative and purposeful endeavors.
6H: Serving others while building wholeness.
7H: Connecting people and building relationships.
8H: Deep transformation and leveraging assets.
9H: Synthesizing diverse information for a new vision.
10H: Influencing others through my work.
11H: Bringing in people for a social cause and humanitarian ideals.
12H: Uncovering deepest secrets and truths for the restoration of self.

3. Modality
If you have a Cardinal Sun sign, you want to make sure that you are creating opportunities for you that allow you to think of the big ideas that allow you to start projects. Now, if you don't have a lot of fixed energy in your charts, you're definitely going to want to get somebody to help you delegate all of those, all of those things that need execution and production.

If your Sun sign is Fixed, you are the problem solver. Make sure that you're creating opportunities that allow you to investigate, allow you to research, and allow you to dig deep. Now, you may need some help with going with the flow. So make sure you build a lot of flexibility into your rigid schedules.

If your Sun sign is in a Mutable sign, you can see all of the different perspectives. Use your wisdom to go with the flow and change your mind. Allow your creative expertise to be seen as an advisor that can see a bird's eye view of things and understand different points-of-view..

4. Element

We have Fire, Water, Air, and Earth, and we know that we want to work within the strength of our elements.

If you have a Fire Sun, you know that you are full of passion and full of energy and full of creativity. So be sure to create opportunities for you that allow you to bring all of that energy, bring all of that fire to your work.

If you have a Water Sun sign, it's a healing, a nurturing and an emotional element. So you'll be wanting to create opportunities that allow you to heal, to nurture, to be empathetic, to be emotional.

If you have an Air Sun sign, remember that air is about connecting with people, it's about learning, it's about intellect, it's a really social element. So you'll want to create opportunities that allow you to be social, allow you to connect, allow you to think, and have fun with your intellectual pursuits.

If your Sun sign is in an Earth sign, make sure that you're trading opportunities that allow you to be embodied, allow you to be practical, allow you to be physical. Earth signs are a receptive sign, and it's all about practicality and getting things done.

5. Aspects

Is your Sun's creative expression in relation to other planetary energies? These other energies can specify your superpowers.

Planetary energy cheat sheet (find the zodiacs and look for planetary rulers for more info)

Sun = Creative vitality
Moon = Emotions and sensing
Mercury = Thoughts and communication
Venus = Connectedness and values
Mars = Energy and drive
Jupiter = Vision and expansion
Saturn = Structure and contraction
Uranus = Breakthrough and innovation
Neptune = Spirituality and imagination
Pluto = Distillation and intensity

Aspect energy cheat sheet (Refer to Major Aspects in How to easily read your chart for more)

Conjunction = Blended with another energy
Opposition = needs integration with another energy
Square = Creative tension with another energy
Trine = Harmonious flow with another energy

REVEAL YOUR SUN'S SUPERPOWERS

Decipher your Sun:

1. What is the sign, quality, and element of your Sun?

Aquarius, fixed air

2. What expertise/mastery does this add to your business?

3. What is the house placement of your Sun?

6th house Sun

4. I express my brand's creative expression in the field of:

5. What area of your business could benefit from more super-power?

6. Does your Sun have any major aspects?

7. What do these aspects help you understand about what you do?

ACTIVATE YOUR SUN'S SUPERPOWERS IN YOUR BRAND

Use your Sun in your business:

1. What exactly do I do?

2. What makes what you do different and better than others?

3. What (work) do you do that feels so easy and not like work?

4. I'm at my best when I'm doing exactly this.

5. In what area of my business does my work shine most?

6. What past experiences, not related to my current role, flavor how I approach my work?

7. What of my past work have others comment as being exceptional?

8. To amplify my creative force, what kind of opportunities do I need to create for myself?

9. To harness and further my mastery, what offer(s) do I need to culminate more of?

10. If I could define my superpower secret sauce, what would it be?

YOUR MOON SIGN

Illuminate Your Brand's Soft Power

MOON SIGN IN YOUR BRAND

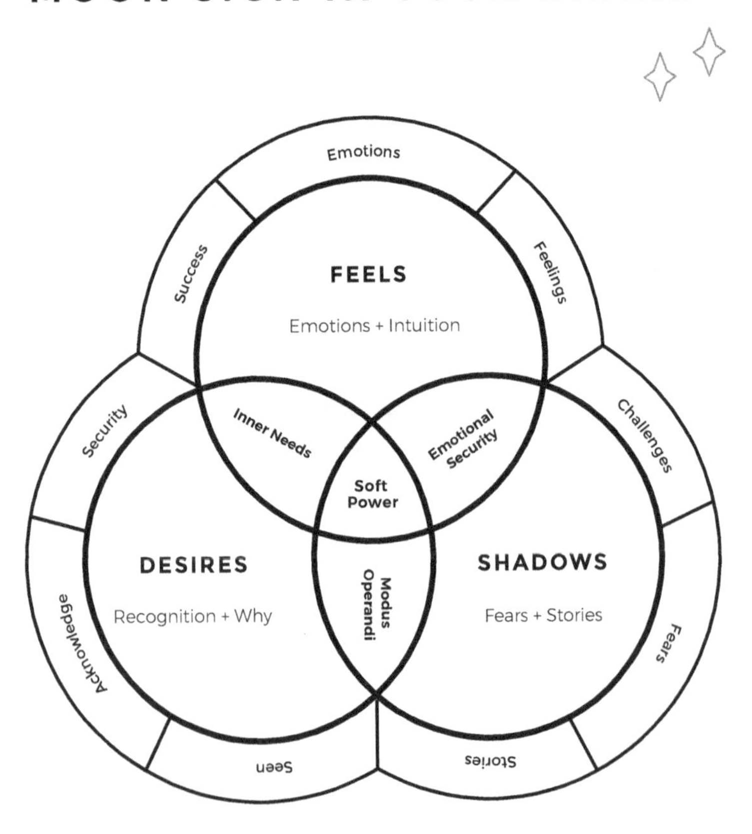

Your Moon sign is part of your brand that others won't necessarily see, but they will certainly feel.

Our Moon sign represents our inner desires, emotions, intuition, as well as parts of us that need healing and extra TLC—our soft powers.

Most of us have been taught that our soft powers don't have a place in business. Our intuition, to not be trusted; our emotions being too much; or our desires, not worthy enough. So instead we turn off our intuition, we repress our emotions and we adopt desires based on what others tell us we "should" want.

By not acknowledging or accepting our soft powers, we are only operating at half capacity!

When we truly understand the power of our intuition to help us make decisions—our emotions to help us discern our own definition of success and recognition—we can operate from a place of wholeness, from a place of authenticity.

And when we are operating from this centered authentic place from within us, others notice!

Our Moon sign helps us to get rooted in our authenticity and guide us through our deep inner-landscape, so we can get to the heart of why we chose this path of entrepreneurship.

Imagine knowing what you truly want and desire in and from your business.

Feels:
I recognize and acknowledge my authentic soft power.

- What you need to feel successful
- Emotional intelligence that motivates you
- Intuitive insight that guides you
- What you need to feel secure

Desires:
I deeply know what I desire from my business and what motivates me.

- What you truly want
- How you want to be recognized
- How you define success
- How you want to be acknowledged

Shadows:
I acknowledge my challenges and I am able to move through them without getting stuck.

- Current challenges and roadblocks
- Inherited fears and past hurts
- Triggers and patterns of stuckness
- Stories that no longer serve you

5 WAYS TO USE YOUR MOON SIGN IN YOUR BUSINESS

✧ **Secure Your Emotions**

When you feel emotionally secure, it becomes a foundation from which you express yourself in business. Your emotional security becomes your anchor—the rooted connection to your inner-knowing. And one of your draws to your soul customers. Your customers will not remember what you say, they will remember how you feel because it makes them feel great!

✧ **Trust Your Intuition**

When we learn to hear our intuition and discern it from emotional fear, we can let it guide us to making choices based on faith versus making choices based on fear. Our intuition is always communicating to us through our body and senses as well as showing us external signs. Most of us have been taught to not trust our intuition. And when we can learn to begin to trust our intuition, rooted in our Moon sign, we can hold space to trust our intuition to make decisions best for our highest selves and business..

✧ **Face Your Fears**

We all need great courage in business. Courage isn't the absence of fear. Instead, it's taking action even when we are scared. If we don't face our fears, we will get stuck and unconsciously operate from the shadow expression of our Moon sign. When we are able to understand and move through our fears, we are able to take the risks we need to go after what we want and succeed.

✧ **Choose Your Destiny**

Your Moon sign shows us what needs nurturing and care in ourselves. She shows us how we desire to be recognized and what success means to us individually. If we don't choose how we want to be seen, others will choose for us, and it's almost always wrong. When you understand what you truly desire, you can claim what recognition and success means to you and declare that outwardly to choose your own destiny.

✧ **Live Your Why**

When you can understand why you do what you do and share that in the world with your brand story, you can call in your ideal customers. All of the meaning in your Moon sign gives you keys to understanding your why. Your why is the seed to your meaning and brand story that brings in your soul customers.

SOFT POWER YOUR MOON SIGN

1. Zodiac Sign

This is the core archetypal energy that you need to nourish and care for in yourself.

Recognize and nurture this feeling and desire through your business. Understand both the light and shadows to gain further insight into your motivations so you can steer your motivations past old patterns into patterns for success.

2. House Placements

Whichever house your Moon is in will give you insight as to what area of your business your emotional and intuitive desires want to be recognized and where you have more soft power to cultivate.

This is where in your biz you need to express your desires and access to healing:

1H: I lead and guide with my emotions/intuition.
2H: I build value with my emotions/intuition.
3H: I promote and communicate with my emotions/intuition.
4H: I root and belong with my emotions/intuition.
5H: I celebrate and create with my emotions/intuition.
6H: I serve and practice with my emotions/intuition.
7H: I connect and relate with my emotions/intuition.
8H: I trust and heal with my emotions/intuition.
9H: I believe and see with my emotions/intuition.
10H: I promise and deliver with my emotions/intuition.
11H: I impact and change with my emotions/intuition.
12H: I surrender and flow with my emotions/intuition.

3. Modality

If you have a Cardinal Moon sign, you want to feel like you can take charge and take initiative. You may want to be recognized as the change maker.

If your Moon sign is Fixed, you want to feel like you are a problem solver. You may want to be acknowledged for your deep expertise.
If your Moon sign is in a Mutable sign, you want to feel free to change your mind. You may want to be appreciated as a sage visionary.

4. Element

We have Fire, Water, Air, and Earth, we know that we want to intuit and feel the strength of our Moon sign element.

If you have a Fire Moon, your intuition may inspire you when you are exerting energy, creating or doing something you're passionate about. Cultivate fiery energy to tap into your inner-knowing. Try activating your intuition with fire or candle gazing.

If you have a Water Moon, your intuition may speak through you when you are in place of stillness. You're already very emotional, intuitive and yes, psychic. Trust in that voice that is already always speaking through you. Understand her as a strength, not a weakness, even if someone in the past has told you your tears are too much. Your tears are your soft power coming through. Your deep emotional well is powerful. Try activating your intuition with water, being by or in water (showers/baths, oceans, lakes, streams).

If you have an Air Moon, your intuition may trigger like an electrical pulse through your body, or an idea suddenly implanted in your mind's eye. You sense a knowing. You may hear sounds or vibrations, you may hear words or songs in the wind. You may not be as emotional as others but you are far from indifferent, your feelings are unusual so they are harder to understand from others. Others can't teach you your own emotional language. Try activating your intuition with air, feeling the breeze on your skin, through your hair, repeating mantras, singing bowls or other vibrational sound work.

If you have an Earth Moon, your intuition is sensed through your entire body. Sometimes your inner knowing feels like calm warmth emanating from your center. Your feet may feel firmly rooted, like you're in slow motion when things feel just right. When you touch a person you feel peace, you know they are the right one. When you pick up something at the store and feel in your body that you need that artifact to help you with something, trust your senses. Smell and touch are only some of your superpowers. Try activating your intuition with Earth, ground your bare feet on Mother Earth, try pottery, gardening, stretching your body.

5. Aspects

Is your Moon's emotional, intuitive soft powers in relation to other planetary energies? These other energies can specify your soft powers.

Planetary energy cheat sheet (find the zodiacs and look for planetary rulers for more info)

Sun = Creative vitality
Moon = Emotions and sensing
Mercury = Thoughts and communication
Venus = Connectedness and values
Mars = Energy and drive
Jupiter = Vision and expansion
Saturn = Structure and contraction
Uranus = Breakthrough and innovation
Neptune = Spirituality and imagination
Pluto = Distillation and intensity

Aspect energy cheat sheet (Refer to Major Aspects in How to easily read your chart for more)

Conjunction = Blended with another energy
Opposition = Needs integration with another energy
Square = Creative tension with another energy
Trine = Harmonious flow with another energy

REVEAL YOUR MOON'S SOFT POWERS

Decipher your Moon:

1. What is the sign, quality and element of your Moon?

Virgo, mutable earth

2. What insight about yourself does this add to your business?

3. What is the house placement of your Moon?

1st house moon

4. I express my brand's desires, needs and attention in field of:

5. What area of your business could benefit from more soft power?

6. Does your moon have any major aspects?

7. What do these aspects help you understand about yourself?

ACTIVATE YOUR MOON'S SOFT POWERS IN YOUR BUSINESS

Use your Moon in your business:

1. How do I want to feel in my business?

2. What does my intuition feel like in my body?

3. How do I desire to be seen in my business?

4. What does success and recognition feel/look like for me in my business?

5. Why did I start my business and become a spiritual entrepreneur

6. Why am I motivated to be successful in my business?

7. What fears am I now aware of this fear/shadow expression of my moon?

8. When I feel this fear, how do I recognize the trigger?

9. When I recognize the trigger, what can I do to move through and release the fear?

10. What could I accomplish if I was able to move through my fear?

Elevate Your Brand's Charm Power

CHARM POWER

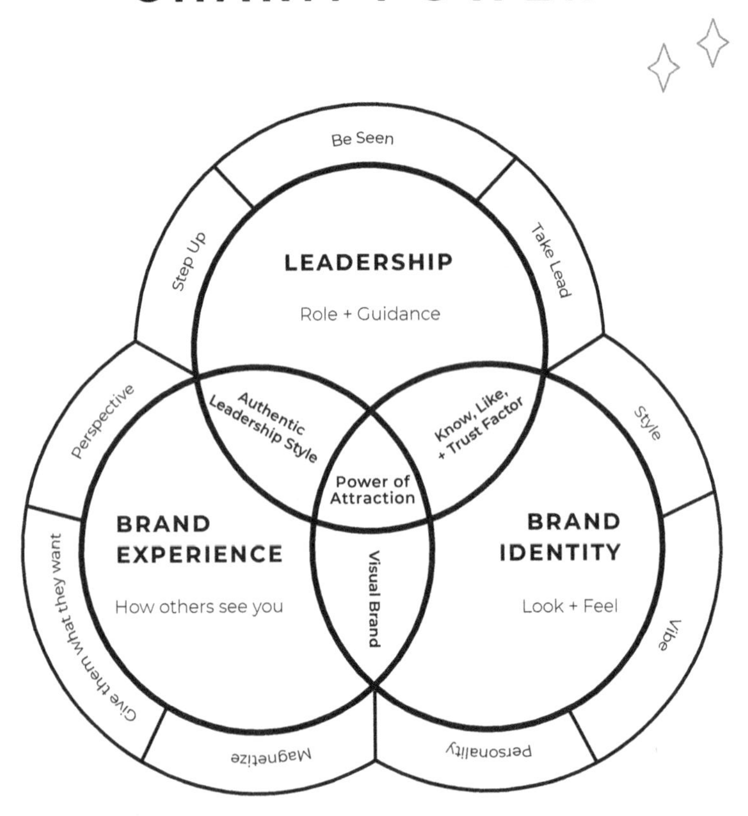

Your Rising sign is the part of your brand that everyone sees! It's the way others already perceive us, the way we are meant to guide others, and the way we are meant to take initiative in our brand.

Your Rising sign represents your brand visibility, brand identity, and your leadership style. Your charm power.

Most of us spend years fine tuning our brand, guessing at what traits we need to bring to the fore, getting stuck in a cycle of comparison or copying.

At the moment we took our first breath, from the exact place on the earth there was a zodiac rising on the eastern horizon, this is your Rising sign. And the energy of your Rising sign, to me, is the most powerful (ancient astrologers put much more weight on this sign than any other in forecasting someone's life).

It's the energy that others already perceive of us. So when we can meet our customers and understand how they already see us, what power would that provide in helping you discover your brand identity and even more, the way you are meant to take lead?

You are here to be a powerful agent of change—a leader in your community and beyond.

With your Sun sign, we illuminated your ultimate superpowers and defined what you have to offer that is unique.

Then we uncovered, with your Moon sign, how you truly desire to be seen and appreciated in order to feel emotionally secure to do the scary things, like being seen in the world.

Now it's time to step into your power by becoming the leader you are meant to be—by becoming the guide that others already see you as.

It's not easy seeing yourself from the outside. Now you can, with your Rising sign.

Imagine knowing how others already perceive you and becoming the best version of that energy to lead others.

Guide You Are Meant to Be

I am a powerful spiritual entrepreneur as I lead others

- Step up
- Be seen
- Take lead

How Others See You

I see how others experience me and I step into that role

- Brand experience
- Outside perspective
- Ideal customer magnetization

Brand Identity

I love being seen as imperfectly perfect me

- Brand personality
- Brand style and design
- Brand vibe

Note: You must know your time and place of birth to calculate your Rising sign. If you do not know this, find a rectification astrologer to help you discover your time of birth. Or better yet, use your intuition when reading the descriptions of Rising signs.

5 WAYS TO MAGNETIZE YOUR BRAND WITH YOUR RISING SIGN

✧ **Genuinely Guide**

Show up consistently as your type of leader as specified by your Rising sign. There are many types of guides to many types of heroes (your ideal customers). It's your job to discover the guide you are meant to be, show up consistently, and contribute to your community. As a business owner or a personal brand, you are an ignitor of new ideas, a creator of valuable content, and a thought leader sharing your vision with your world. Step into your power.

Lead by being:

- ♈ **Aries Rising** – A born leader, who's adventurous and courageous
- ♉ **Taurus Rising** - An easy going, charming, and pleasure-seeking guide
- ♊ **Gemini Rising:** Well-informed, knows-a-lot-of-things teacher and storyteller
- ♋ **Cancer Rising:** Motherly, loving, and empathetic safe-space creatrix
- ♌ **Leo Rising:** Creative, heart-centered, and inspirational performer
- ♍ **Virgo Rising:** Analytical, organized, and health-nut overachiever
- ♎ **Libra Rising:** Peaceful warrior and connector
- ♏ **Scorpio Rising:** Intense, transformative counselor
- ♐ **Sagittarius Rising:** Freedom-loving, optimistic, and visionary trend-setter
- ♑ **Capricorn Rising:** Practical, goal-oriented enterprise builder
- ♒ **Aquarius Rising:** Innovative, tech-forward humanitarian
- ♓ **Pisces Rising:** Spiritual, relaxed, and intuitive coach

✧ **Attract your Ideal Customer**

Step into your leadership style and become an irresistible magnet to your ideal soul customers. Your Rising sign, by polarity, attracts those who embody the energy of zodiac on the other side of your chart. Your soul customers will have the aspirations and fears of the opposite sign (descendant), they will not necessarily "be" that sign. Be aware that we often project the shadow side of our descendant, that energy will feel familiar to you. You do not need to operate as your descendant. Instead, step into the power of your rising and focus your leadership energies there.

Your Rising - Your Polarity (aka Descendant)

Aries ——— Libra
Taurus ——— Scorpio
Gemini ——— Sagittarius
Cancer ——— Capricorn
Leo ——— Aquarius
Virgo ——— Pisces
Libra ——— Aries
Scorpio ——— Taurus
Sagittarius ——— Gemini
Capricorn ——— Cancer
Aquarius ——— Leo
Pisces ——— Virgo

✧ **Get Focused**

Know your strengths, know your priorities with laser focus, and get help with all the rest. Whether it's outsourcing, hiring, or delegating to your VA (Virtual Assistant) those unimportant tasks you've been busying yourself with, your Rising sign will point to the tasks you need to focus on to best use your energy and the tasks you need to reapportion.

✧ **Get Productive**

Start your day with the themes of your Rising sign. This routine sets you up with easy accomplishments at the beginning of your day so you continue on that productive trajectory.

✧ **Get Personal**

Use your Rising sign to inform your brand identity and personality so it aligns with your authentic leadership style and attracts your ideal audience—everything from your marketing materials' look and feel, to how you package things across your brand touchpoints. Your Rising sign is the starting point for all your collateral's visuals and messaging: logo, website, printed materials, pitch decks, decor, and more!

CHARM POWER YOUR RISING SIGN

1. ZODIAC SIGN

This is the core archetypal energy that you need to lead and show up as. Stretch into this role and lead from this energy. Create your brand identity and visuals from this energy as well. All your future first steps and initiative will want to incorporate this energy.

♈ **Aries Rising: A born leader, who's adventurous and courageous**
Brands with Aries Rising need to show up as natural, decisive leaders. You may act before thinking things through, but that's why people follow you—because of your fiery drive. You have a clear vision of what you want and don't really want to hear others opinions. You do best when you are able to persuade your people to get onboard with your ideas; you can't be a leader if you have no followers. You lead well from a place of passion, and you are expressive as hell. You want to be noticed but use your competitiveness in constructive non-belligerent ways. (Look in the Archetype Reference for detailed information on Aries.)

Lead by:
- Being confident and bold
- Making quick decisions
- Persuading people to buy into your idea

♉ **Taurus Rising: An easygoing, charming, and pleasure-seeking guide**
Brands with Taurus Rising need to show up grounded, centered, and peaceful. Yes, you may take time to do things in your specific (and practical) way, but that's because nothing beautiful has ever happened in a rush. You enjoy and even create life's pleasures, as these give you and your customers a sense of security. If your business was

a farm, it would involve an on-trend, boho farmhouse next to a lush meadow perfect for influencer photos of your craft goods. You lead with a can-do presence. Abundance is key for you, but be sure you manage your resources and don't accumulate selfishly. (Look in the Archetype Reference for detailed information on Taurus.)

Lead by:

- ✧ Being strong and able-bodied
- ✧ Creating comfort and physical security
- ✧ Radiating calm, centered self-worth

♊ Gemini Rising: Well-informed, knows-a-lot-of-things teacher and storyteller

Brands with Gemini Rising need to show up as well-rounded, multi-skilled Janes of all trades. You know a lot about a lot, and you do well when you are sharing this knowledge with like-minded people. Guide others through your speaking, writing, and storytelling. Your adaptability and versatility make your presence a game changer in any crisis. Use your humor and wit for good, and catch your tongue when it gets too talkative. People are listening to you, so take a stance, even if you can see every side. Lead with your voice,, and slow down once in a while to gather your thoughts so you can spread your message. (Look in the Archetype Reference for detailed information on Gemini.)

Lead by:

- ✧ Spinning animated stories and narratives that communicate your vision
- ✧ Creating a dialogue with your community that engages their buy-in
- ✧ Adapting quickly to the chaos of the now--nothing will stop you

♋ Cancer Rising: Motherly, loving, and empathetic safe-space creatrix

Brands with Cancer Rising need to show up as nurturing leaders. You lead with kindness, the eternal cheerleader. Your encouraging words are the rewards your people need to continue forward. You are a compassionate, empathetic leader in your family, community, and the world at large, as you create a safe space for others' true transformation to occur. People need to be aware that even though you are kind hearted to the core, your fierce protective claws will come out at any provocation to your community. Be sure that your protective nature doesn't go too far, and choose your battles wisely. (Look in the Archetype Reference for detailed information on Cancer.)

Lead by:

- Being tolerant and kind to all
- Creating safe spaces for change to occur
- Showing kindness and forgiveness to self

♌ Leo Rising: Creative, heart-centered, and inspirational performer

Brands with Leo Rising need to show up as a lively, happy leader. You are an effervescent creative force, and no one can tell you how to be the boss. When you are working from the heart, doing things that light you up, you draw people in like the Luminary you are. If you don't operate from this place of passion, your light dulls and your flair for being center stage turns dark. If this happens, take a break and shake out your slump until you can get back on stage and lead again from the heart. Leo Rising is also the sign of Royalty, but only sovereigns that have a spark of joy in their eye win the hearts of their followers. (Look in the Archetype Reference for detailed information on Leo.)

Lead by:

- Following your heart, because passion is a key to your success
- Doing work that is joyful to you; if it's not joyful, delegate it to someone else
- Creating opportunities for you to show off a bit. Fireworks? Yes!

♍ Virgo Rising: Analytical, organized, and health-nut overachiever

Brands with Virgo Rising need to show up as leaders that are put together, efficient, and of service. You paint a picture of perfection and wholeness, and people truly admire your dedication and your example. You are the embodiment of an earth mother, one that feeds her body and soul and teaches others to do the same. You may be involved in work that includes nature, holistic services, or health. You can do equally well surrounded by spreadsheets or to-do lists. But this desire to be a perfect and efficient leader can take its toll as you can become stuck in striving for an unattainable ideal. It's important for you to have clear boundaries. When you feel the urge to continue working after you've passed your limit, remember your need for wholeness and self-care. You can't lead effectively when you are depleted. (Look in the Archetype Reference for detailed information on Virgo.)

Lead by:

- Keeping your body healthy and whole—you are one with your body and operate only when it's in tip top form (this extends to all your physical and emotional spaces too)
- Analyzing situations for efficiency and productivity
- Being extremely helpful, with service at your core

♎ Libra Rising: Peaceful warrior and connector

Brands with Libra Rising need to show up as people-loving leaders. You are here to stand for peace at any cost and to lead by creating beauty in the world through your own personal style or creations. You are a leader that others are drawn to and you love inter-connecting people from your many circles. Partnerships, affiliate programs, and networking with other business leaders are at the heart of your success. You can not operate in isolation. But be aware of maintaining your leadership because in your desire to please others, you can over-give and lose yourself. Notice if you are avoiding conflict at the expense of doing what's right for your business. (Look in the Archetype Reference for detailed information on Libra.)

Lead by:

- Being a friendly social butterfly
- Drawing in the right people to partner with you
- Creating beauty or peace where there was none

♏ Scorpio Rising: Intense, transformative counselor

Brands with Scorpio Rising need to show up as leaders that catalyze deep transformation. You have immense power that needs to be used to benefit yourself as well as the others that you serve. You have the ability to lead by digging into the deepest issues that prevent trust. You work well counseling others on taboo topics like sex, money and addictions—anything to do with one's ability or inability to exert power and control. Rather than keeping your cards close to you in secrecy, find those that you can truly trust. You have sex appeal and you can use it! If you feel a bit shy, start off with a sweep of red lipstick and sexy librarian glasses. This appeal will help you cultivate your status as a power player. (Look in the Archetype Reference for detailed information on Scorpio.)

Lead by:

- Using your innate power to empower others
- Learning to trust yourself and the people that have proved themselves
- Understanding that your depth of emotion is a gift that you can tap into

♐ Sagittarius Rising: Freedom-loving, optimistic, and visionary trend setter

Brands with Sagittarius Rising need to show up as inspirational! You get people riled up with the excitement of possibility with your sheer optimism and love. You are one that is never in one place long, always looking for the next adventure. Even if you are an atypical home-bound Sagittarius, you often journey to far off places in your life-long learnings and spiritual explorations. You work well when you are leading by sharing your knowledge and inspiring others to create their own version of a life of freedom. You love hearing your own voice but be wary of staying on your soapbox for too long. You have the gift of big vision. The challenge is to define this big picture in our earthly realm so others understand your purpose. (Look in the Archetype Reference for detailed information on Sagittarius.)

Lead by:

- Inspiring others by sharing your vast knowledge
- Give gratitude for everything that comes your way
- Creating a freedom life that allows you to ever-explore

♑ Capricorn Rising: Practical, goal-oriented enterprise builder

Brands with Capricorn Rising need to show up as a professional business leader. You give off an air of authority and integrity. You are ambitious and goal-oriented; there isn't anything that you put your mind to that you cannot do. You work well when you are disciplined and have a great structure. As a goaldigger, be sure to be socially responsible. As you achieve, be sure that you are going after things you want, not something that someone else wants for you. And realize that while you have a clear goal in your mind, you won't be able to control others to do your bidding unless you include them in the goal. (Look in the Archetype Reference for detailed information on Capricorn.)

Lead by:

- Presenting yourself professionally, have accreditations? Use them.
- Always having a goal in mind
- Achieving for yourself in a way that is sustainable for all

♒ Aquarius Rising: Innovative, tech-forward humanitarian

Brands with Aquarius Rising need to show up as futuristic thought leaders with utopia on their agenda. You are a friendly leader as you are curious about what makes the other person tick. But when people get too emotionally needy, you're out the door. You are a rebel wanting to shake things up and do things in your own way. Your liberal and innovative ideals can work to progress all of humanity, but be sure that you aren't too ahead of your time. Your need to be different can work against you; if you deem yourself a lone wolf, you will never be able to accomplish your goals without your people. Come back to the present to understand where people are at now in order to take them to your place in the future. (Look in the Archetype Reference for detailed information on Aquarius.)

Lead by:

- Being uniquely you
- Being friendly and widening your network
- Being a changemaker in your field

♓ **Pisces Rising: Spiritual, relaxed, and intuitive coach**
Brands with Pisces Rising need to show up as imaginative and intuitive big-picture thinkers, who lead through spirit. Your compassionate soul is an asset to be protected as your porous and giving nature will attract those only wanting to take. Wisdom and metaphor is your language, as you are a 10,000 year old soul. You are able to connect people into imaginative tales about your big visions—who has time for details and plans? Trust that you will be inspired daily to strategically get you to where you need to be to accomplish your big vision. The details of a thorough plan can get too heavy and may sink you. (Look in the Archetype Reference for detailed information on Pisces.)

Lead by:
- Letting go of unnecessary things and circumstances
- Relaxing and bring more imaginative flow into your work
- Intuiting what you and others really need right here and now

2. Ruler of your Rising's House Placement
Your leadership ability is best utilized when it is directed in the area of your business, by house, to where your Rising sign planet is located.

1. Find the planetary ruler of your Rising sign

SIGN	PLANETARY RULER
♈ Aries	♂ Mars
♉ Taurus	♀ Venus
♊ Gemini	☿ Mercury
♋ Cancer	☽ Moon
♌ Leo	☉ Sun
♍ Virgo	☿ Mercury
♎ Libra	♀ Venus
♏ Scorpio	♇ Pluto + ♂ Mars
♐ Sagittarius	♃ Jupiter
♑ Capricorn	♄ Saturn
♒ Aquarius	♅ Uranus + ♄ Saturn
♓ Pisces	♆ Neptune + ♃ Jupiter

2. In your natal chart, discover the house that your ruler occupies to direct your leadership ability in your business.

1H: Focus your leadership on your personal development, you are self-motivated and self-interested (not selfish).
2H: Focus your leadership on your self-worth, creating wealth, and resource contribution, possessions.
3H: Focus your leadership on communicating your ideas, writings, speaking, graphic design.
4H: Focus your leadership on creating safe communities and spaces, creating emotional security. Maybe there's an element of a family business or legacy too.
5H: Focus your leadership with play, creativity, performance, and young or young at heart.
6H: Focus your leadership in the area of efficiency, health, wholeness, daily routines, and systems.
7H: Focus your leadership in the area of partnerships, affiliations, close networks, and great 1:1 relationships.
8H: Focus your leadership on handling other people's money or resources, or transforming, others at a deep level through counseling or therapy.
9H: Focus your leadership on promoting vision, online marketing, expanding faith and international reach.
10H: Focus your leadership on business, career, or elevating your authority in the public eye.
11H: Focus your leadership on social impact networks, platforms, and extended community building.
12H: Focus your leadership on creating retreats or more ease in business. You may work with healing or subconscious modalities too.

3. Modality
If you have a Cardinal Rising sign, you take lead by being in charge, taking initiative and being first.

If your Rising sign is Fixed, you take lead by uncovering truths, diving deep, and solving complex problems.

If your Rising sign is in a Mutable sign, you take lead by bringing in diverse ideas together to create an inspirational win-win situation.

4. Element

If you have a Fire Rising, your brand identity needs to be inspiring and creative.

If you have a Water Rising, your brand identity needs to be healing and nurturing.

If you have an Air Rising, your brand identity needs to be thought provoking and social.

If you have an Earth Rising, your brand identity needs to focus on building and sustaining.

5. Other Energies in Your First House

Your leadership style and brand identity if modified by other energies that exist in your first house. Are there other energies that you need to add to your leadership style?

Add these energies to your leadership style and brand identity if you have them in the first house:

Sun = Creative vitality
Moon = Emotions and sensing
Mercury = Thoughts and communication
Venus = Connectedness and values
Mars = Energy and drive
Jupiter = Vision and expansion
Saturn = Structure and contraction
Uranus = Breakthrough and innovation
Neptune = Spirituality and imagination
Pluto = Distillation and intensity

REVEAL YOUR RISING SIGN'S POWER OF ATTRACTION

Decipher your Rising:

1. What is the sign, quality and element of your Rising sign?

Leo, fixed fire

2. What insight about yourself does this add to your leadership style?

3. What is the house placement of the ruling planet of your Rising?

4. What area of your business could benefit from authentic leadership and initiative?

5. Does your first house have any additional planets?

moon & pluto

6. What do these added energies add to your Power of Attraction?

ACTIVATE YOUR RISING'S ATTRACTION POWERS IN YOUR BRAND

1. My leadership style is...

2. My leadership is best directed in this area of my business...

3. I must show up and guide like this to be more relatable and authentic...

4. I start my day to be productive by...

5. My brand identity currently aligns with the energy of my Rising sign in this way...

6. I need to stretch into my Rising energy by filling these gaps in my brand identity...

7. My brand personality needs to feel...

8. People love this about my brand identity...

9. My brand visuals need to include more of this feeling...

10. My ideal customers embody this astro-graphic energy...

11. My ideal customers have these core aspirations and fears...

YOUR ASTROBRAND™ MAP

Put it all together and let this serve as your compass rose to position your business.

- **My Superpower**

  I love doing and am freaking great at...

  I am an expert in...

  I have a unique approach...

  I multiply these opportunities to work my genius...

✧ My Soft Power

I want to be recognized as...

I define success in business as...

My why and motivation operandi to being a spiritual entrepreneur is...

✧ My Charm Power

I am this kind of leader...

I take this kind of initiative in this area of my brand...

My brand personality and identity is...

CLOSING WORDS

I do believe your soul chose to be born at a specific time with the imprint of the energies of our solar system weaved into your energy.

Your core foundational energies are the heart and soul of who you are and what you were put here to do on this earth.

There are many other beautiful shiny objects in the solar system to give more specificity to your AstroBrand™. The temptation to get distracted by every little asteroid and outer planet is there. Return to your Sun, Moon, and Rising; your core frequencies.

They need to be fine tuned regularly to reflect upon how your free will and life experiences shift your outer expressionsions in your business. Your core energy can elevate and evolve with the way you express yourself in your work. Check in to see if you need a bit of realignment.

Like a well-tuned guitar or orchestra, the sound vibrates in harmony and resonates, carrying it's beautiful melodies and energies further.

You are the orchestra. The more intune you are with your core energies, the more effectively your energy will carry outward into the world.

It's all in you. In your star-powered design.

RESOURCES

GET YOUR CHART

You can get free charts from

Astro.com

Astro-charts.com

I am not affiliated with any of these sites.

ABOUT THE AUTHOR

I'm Leslie Tagorda (she/her), a multiracial, brand astrologer, and strategist. An Aquarius boss woman and Human Design Projector, I call myself a Brand Navigator as I guide transformational visionaries to reach for and exceed their expectations using my own system of an empowered brand and biz astrology called The AstroBrand Method™.

Since 2004 I've helped hundreds of entrepreneurs and social impact organizations clarify their brand story, express themselves through their websites, social and brands so they can stop hiding and shine brighter like the luminaries they are meant to be.

I host a podcast and Facebook community The Savvy Luminary – Astrology for Entrepreneurs. And when not stargazing and advising, I'm a professional classical clarinetist touring with my nationally-recognized chamber ensemble or playing in the pits of groups like the San Francisco Ballet and the San Francisco Opera.

I currently reside in the occupied land of the Ohlone Ramaytush currently called San Francisco with my husband and son.

- Listen to my weekly astrology for entrepreneurs podcast on your favorite podcast player: The Savvy Luminary
- Schedule a breakthrough AstroBrand™ session where we chart your star-powered brand and position it exactly to your design (leadership role, true values, ideal customer astrographics (archetype + psychographics), brand visibility and communication style- I can see all of this in your chart) Newmooncreative.co/astrobrand

 Podcast: TheSavvyLuminary.com

 Instagram: @newmooncreativeco

 Facebook Group: facebook.com/groups/TheSavvyLuminary

 Youtube: youtube.com/c/NewMoonCreativeCo